MW01532443

Deeper Yet
Meditations for the Quiet Hour

By
Clarence E. Eberman
Pastor of the Moravian Church, Lancaster,
Penn., and President of the Pennsylvania
Christian Endeavor Union

With Preface By
Rev. Floyd W. Tomkins, D.D.
Rector of Holy Trinity Episcopal
Church, Philadelphia, Penn.

First Fruits Press
Wilmore, Kentucky
c2015

Deeper yet: meditations for the quiet hour, by Clarence E. Eberman

First Fruits Press, ©2015
Previously published: Boston and Chicago: United Society of Christian Endeavor, ©1900.

ISBN: 9781621713555 (print), 9781621713562 (digital)

Digital version at http://place.asburyseminary.edu/christianendeavorbooks/29/

First Fruits Press is a digital imprint of the Asbury Theological Seminary, B.L. Fisher Library. Asbury Theological Seminary is the legal owner of the material previously published by the Pentecostal Publishing Co. and reserves the right to release new editions of this material as well as new material produced by Asbury Theological Seminary. Its publications are available for noncommercial and educational uses, such as research, teaching and private study. First Fruits Press has licensed the digital version of this work under the Creative Commons Attribution Noncommercial 3.0 United States License. To view a copy of this license, visit http://creativecommons.org/licenses/by-nc/3.0/us/.

For all other uses, contact:

First Fruits Press
B.L. Fisher Library
Asbury Theological Seminary
204 N. Lexington Ave.
Wilmore, KY 40390
http://place.asburyseminary.edu/firstfruits

Eberman, Clarence E.
    Deeper yet : meditations for the quiet hour / by Clarence E. Eberman.
    [1] leaf of plates, 128 pages : illustration ; 21 cm.
    Wilmore, Ky. : First Fruits Press, ©2015.
    Reprint. Previously published: Boston: United Society of Christian Endeavor, ©1900.
    ISBN: 9781621713555 (pbk.)
    1. Meditations. 2. Devotional exercises. I. Title.
BV4832 .E3 2015   242.2

Cover design by Jonathan Ramsay

asburyseminary.edu
800.2ASBURY
204 North Lexington Avenue
Wilmore, Kentucky 40390

First Fruits
THE ACADEMIC OPEN PRESS OF ASBURY SEMINARY

First Fruits Press
The Academic Open Press of Asbury Theological Seminary
204 N. Lexington Ave., Wilmore, KY 40390
859-858-2236
first.fruits@asburyseminary.edu
asbury.to/firstfruits

CHRIST IN GETHSEMANE.

From painting by Liska.

Deeper Yet

Meditations for the Quiet Hour

He clave the rocks in the wilderness, and gave them drink as out of the great depths.—Ps. 78: 15.

O the depth of the riches both of the wisdom and knowledge of God !—Rom. 11: 33.

By Clarence E. Eberman

Pastor of the Moravian Church, Lancaster, Penn., and President of the Pennsylvania Christian Endeavor Union

WITH PREFACE BY

REV. FLOYD W. TOMKINS, D. D.

Rector of Holy Trinity Episcopal Church, Philadelphia, Penn.

United Society of Christian Endeavor
Boston and Chicago

Copyright, 1900,
by the
UNITED SOCIETY OF CHRISTIAN ENDEAVOR

DEDICATION

To the Comrades of the Quiet Hour, who have daily
brought their empty chalices to the Eternal Fountain, that they might be filled; who have prayed
for deeper experiences of God's presence,
and who have not waited in vain
upon the Lord in the early
watches of the morning

THIS MESSAGE IS AFFECTIONATELY DEDICATED

with the prayer that
the Spirit of Christ may
constantly lead his disciples into
the mastery of the deepest truths of
the blessed life.

INVOCATION

By thy holy incarnation and birth,
By thy pure and blameless childhood,
By thy obedience, diligence, and faithfulness,
By thy humility, meekness, and patience,
By thy faithfulness in thine earthly calling,
By thy perfect life before God and man,
By thy baptism, fasting, and temptation,
By thy griefs and sorrows,
By thy prayers and tears,
By thy having been despised and rejected,
Bless and comfort us, gracious Lord and God.

By thy crown of thorns,
By thy cross and passion,
By thy sacred wounds and precious blood,
By thy atoning death,
By thy rest in the grave,
By thy glorious resurrection and ascension,
By thy sitting at the right hand of God,
By thy sending the Holy Ghost,
By thy prevailing intercession,
By the holy sacraments,
By thy divine presence,
By thy coming again to thy church on earth, or our being called home to thee,
Bless and comfort us, gracious Lord and God.

By thy willing sacrifice of thyself even unto death
Make known to us the mystery of thy love.

Fulfil in us thy prayer that all who love thee may be one,
as thou art in the Father, and the Father in thee.

Preface.

THERE can be no doubt that the greatest need in this bustling, rushing, materialistic, money-making age is a deepening of the normal spiritual life, so that religion shall be to men not merely an acceptance of doctrines, or a connection with a church, but a conscious knowledge of God's presence.

The " practice of the presence of God " was one of the good things of the mediæval age. The Christian world turned from it when the errors of that dark sea were thrown aside, and it is with difficulty that we can come back to it. We are afraid of emotionalism. We dread a possible asceticism which in the strong demands of contemplation may make common duties irksome. Life is so full of energy that we cannot endure the thought of a Christian shutting himself away from human needs and demands while he dreams of strange spiritual ideals.

7

And yet we must recognize that human needs can be adequately met only when we are fired by a conscious power which, coming from above, grants to us wisdom and strength. We find ourselves capable of doing ordinary things only when we see them transfigured by the all-pervading love of God.

Meditation becomes a necessity to a true man just in proportion to his zeal. If he is to be more than a machine, he must see the meaning and order which lies back of the machinery. There must be "the living creature" in the wheels. (Ezek. 1: 21.)

The reason men dislike meditation is largely because in the past it has been subjective. To meditate upon one's self is never productive of much exaltation. The sight of sins and failures calls for self-despite and mortification of the body, sadly considered vile, such as the mediæval saints too frequently indulged in, thinking the destruction of evil the sure path to holiness.

But true meditation must have a lofty and infinite object. To look within is to find despair; to look to God is to find hope.

Our modern contemplation, therefore, rests upon God, upon Jesus Christ, upon the Holy Spirit. Forgetful of himself, the man, like the sick folk in the gospel, fixes his eyes upon Christ. The love, the kindness, the watchful power, the wisdom, of God,—these bring the surest destruction to evil, the surest exaltation of God. To remember that God is near, a constant, personal Friend; to know that we can commune with him unceasingly; to become far-sighted so that we can detect his "ruling hand in each event of life"; to love him with that simple, normal love of a child for his father, which neither runs to wild delirium of excitement, nor rests in gloomy silence, but clings with intense trust,—these are the great parts of a true, healthy religion.

One always rejoices, then, when any effort is made to lead men to this practical Christianity. The world has many books which have given comfort. À Kempis's "Imitation of Christ," Taylor's "Holy Living" and Wilson's "Sacra Privata" have helped hundreds. Yet they are often morbid and abnormal. What is needed is a cheery, bright, hopeful series of meditations, which shall inspire and strengthen.

The "quiet hour" demands helps which

shall not suffer reaction, but which shall rather create a sweet fragrance to last and permeate all the hours.

This book is designed to meet this demand, and experience will doubtless prove its admirable fitness. Its author, a dear friend and brother, has written, as all true men must write, from the depths of his own feeling. It is always an uncovering of personal experience when such a book comes forth; but the revelation, while it enhances the confidence and respect felt for the author, creates a desire to emulate and to seek a like peace.

May God grant his benediction to this book, and cause it to refresh and comfort and inspire thousands.

FLOYD W. TOMKINS.

Holy Trinity Rectory,
Philadelphia, Penn.

CONTENTS

CHAPTER		PAGE
	INVOCATION	3
	DEDICATION	5
	PREFACE	7
I.	THE INCENSE OF PRAYER	13
II.	SEEING JESUS	17
III.	THE GLORY OF SALVATION	21
IV.	THE SURRENDER	25
V.	MUCH MORE	29
VI.	THE THREE CROSSES	33
VII.	THE DIVINE PARTNERSHIP	37
VIII.	GUIDANCE AND GLORY	41
IX.	LOVE'S RESCUE	45
X.	THE VISION OF GOD	49
XI.	THROUGH KNOWLEDGE TO TRUST	53
XII.	THE HIGHER LIFE	57
XIII.	THE STIMULUS OF DEFEAT	61
XIV.	PAUL'S THREE AMBITIONS	65
XV.	LOVE SEEKING LOVE	69
XVI.	THE FORGOTTEN PLACE	73
XVII.	THROUGH THE FIRES	77
XVIII.	GOD'S PROPERTY	81
XIX.	THE DIVINE PATTERN	85
XX.	THE TIME FACTOR	89
XXI.	THE LENS OF PURITY	93
XXII.	GOD'S VIGILANCE	97

12   *CONTENTS.*

CHAPTER   PAGE
XXIII.   IN GOD WE TRUST 101
XXIV.   THE LOST CHORD 105
XXV.   THE GREATER WORKS 109
XXVI.   A THREEFOLD MINISTRY 113
XXVII.   HEART-HYMNS 117
XXVIII.   GOD'S SUMMITS 121
XXIX.   A CONSECRATION HYMN 125

Deeper Yet.

THE INCENSE OF PRAYER.

Let my prayer be set forth before thee as incense; and the lifting up of my hands as the evening sacrifice. —*Ps.* 141 : 2.

TRUE prayer is the Christian's vital breath. It is also as incense before the Lord. We narrow the meaning by thinking that in prayer we only ask for something. Shall we not express our love? Shall we not praise God for his own sake? Shall we not sit at the Master's feet in the school of prayer, and learn of him?

Friends living together are not continually asking favors of one another. More likely, they are making sacrifices, as truest soul-communion expresses itself in unselfish ministry.

The prayer life is always larger than our prayer words. As we walk with Jesus, we shall find that his blessed life will inspire

13

the spirit of true prayer; yea, his presence will start the fountains of our love.

The Holy Spirit seeks continually to revise our prayers, to enlarge them, to give them the true bent heavenwards, and also to make the soul responsive to the divine love.

If the waves of ether will carry earthly messages to a sensitive receiver, how much truer it is that the petitions of God's children will be heard of the Father! But the other side of the truth is supremely important. We speak to God in prayer. He also speaks to us. Do we hear his voice? Are our souls sensitive enough, and still enough, and pure enough, to receive his messages? Is the circuit between our souls and the mercy-seat complete?

On one occasion, the Atlantic cable would not operate. At last, the discovery was made that a small sea-fish had penetrated the insulation and had broken the circuit. Very small things have broken our spiritual contact with the mercy-seat. Trifling objects have come between us and God, and have thwarted the work of grace in our hearts.

The prayer life is the soul living and communing with God. It is fellowship, expressed in trust and love. _ Why do we deceive ourselves by surrounding the blessing of prayer with uncertainty and mystery? It is our privilege to live with our Father, to talk with him, to come to him in our weakness and in our want, and to tell him how much we need him. It is not necessary to know or to understand everything; it is sufficient to love much, and to trust implicitly. We can lay our plans before him, and we can express to him our love for him. We can tell him our failings, our poverty of faith and spirit. We can confess to him the lurking spirit of pride or selfishness, and ask him to overcome for us. We can bring to him all our failures and our defeats. We can come to him in our gladness, and share our happiness with him. We can come to him in our woe; and, as we mingle our tears with our petitions, behold, his love will rainbow a promise on the storm-clouds, and we shall not go to our arduous tasks unblest. "Truly our fellowship is with the Father, and with his Son Jesus Christ." "Truly, they who trust the Lord shall not want."

Soul of mine, how dost thou pray? What

hast thou brought to thy Heavenly Father to-day, an incense prayer or a complaining one, a loving message or a doubting fear? Is thy prayer in the language of love, or is it querulous, fault-finding, formal? Pray that thou mayest pray aright. Offer to God the incense of true prayer before thou canst expect the incense of grace and blessing in return.

Evening has come. The day's work is done or undone. Hast thou lifted up holy hands, or unclean ones, or empty ones, at thy evening sacrifice? What! nothing done, nothing wrought, through the precious moments of the day, now gone forever, to glorify thy Lord, to honor his promises, and to extend his kingdom of love? His grace is so full and free! Hast thou come empty-handed? O, come closer to thy Father God, and, hungering for the spirit of his Son, pray that thou mayest be a better worker on the morrow, if the light of earth dawns for thee in the morning.

SEEING JESUS.

Sir, we would see Jesus.—*John* 12: 21.

T is said that a famous educator, a man of deep piety and earnest faith, had moments of mental depression. On one occasion he entered his class-room very much depressed, and, as was his custom, he knelt in prayer with his students. As he arose from his knees, his face bathed in tears, but radiant with a new-found joy, he exclaimed, "Dear young gentlemen, I have just caught a glimpse of Jesus."

The nameless Greeks of old came to the disciples with this intense desire, that they might see Jesus. The great feast offered them many interesting sights; but their hearts were restless, because they wanted, above all things, a glimpse of Jesus.

The vision of Christ is always more important than even the vision of our duty, because the best service is that which his presence inspires, and to which his voice calls. It is absolutely essential for us to

17

seek occasions when we may lay aside the endeavors and the objects of our strenuous life, and thwart the subtle, overreaching tendency of our self-life, in order that we may simply be conscious of God, of his life, of his presence, of his love.

We are concerned about our service. We know the need of deeper consecration. We seek to inspire one another by our messages. But the blessing comes to us when the vision of Jesus shapes our service, and we can say with the disciples, "We see no man save Jesus only," who has given us his Spirit.

The Master while here upon earth always drew his motives from above. The Father's will shaped and moulded his daily ministry. He will also constrain us to come apart with him, the soul alone with God, in order that our lives may be shaped and inspired through motives which come from him. He knows the strain upon the human heart. He knows the subtlety of the human soul. Life under the impetus of lower motives always converges toward the earth.

The time may come when we think that we are masters, and not disciples; that we are owners of the vineyard, and not God's

husbandmen, not his tillage. The secret
of power is the soul always dependent upon
the divine strength. "When I am weak,
then am I strong."

All that we have and are, we have received from above. "Come unto me, and
I will give." God alone is the Giver. He
is our life, and we are capable of commun-
ion with him. What we are is largely de-
termined by what our faith sees. "We
need the silence of the divine fellowship, in
order that God's life may sink deep into the
soul, and become a part of its inner and
essential life." We cannot see the whole
of life's way; but we can see Jesus, our
Guide, and his blessed face will inspire and
strengthen us for every service.

We need the vision of Jesus to determine
the intensity of our daily living. The vision
of faith transfigures believers into disciples.

Jesus is willing to live with us in our
homes. Let this be the motto:—

> " Jesus, the head of this house,
>   The unseen guest at every meal,
>   The silent listener to every conversation."

Jesus is willing to live with us in our
hearts. Open, open to him, and he will

abide.　How can we go wrong when, looking into his blessed face, we are guided by
his presence ?　How can we possibly cher-
ish sin, and still look into his blessed eyes ?

My brother, the secret of the Christian
life is not that we see Jesus now and then,
but that we live with him, that we walk
with him, that we hear his voice summon-
ing us to hourly fellowship and a moment-
by-moment discipleship.　May the Lord
richly reveal himself to thee in the quiet
hour, and send thee forth to bear for him
the burdens of the busy hour.

> " Gaze one moment on the Face whose beauty
> 　Wakes the world's great hymn ;
> Feel it one unutterable moment
> 　Bent in love o'er him.
> In that look feel heaven, earth, men, and angels
> 　Distant grow and dim.
> In that look feel heaven, earth, men, and angels
> 　Nearer grow through him."

The Glory of Salvation.

Help us, O God of our salvation, for the glory of thy name; and deliver us, and purge away our sins, for thy name's sake.—*Ps.* 79 : 9.

SALVATION is more than the rescue of the human soul. The angels sung the key-note of salvation on the first Christmas morn, "Glory to God in the highest." Salvation is a revelation of God's glory.

God has no pleasure in the death of the wicked. "Turn ye, turn ye, why will ye die?" There is grief in the Father's heart over every erring child of his who wilfully wanders away from home.

Sin is an intruder. Like a plague that withers and devastates, so sin is the enemy of peace and righteousness.

The Son of God came to destroy the works of the evil one. The solitudes of the wilderness, the deep shades of the olive garden, the agony of Calvary, tell us the intensity and the dreadfulness of the battle.

Harbored sin leads to inevitable ruin.

"Thou hast destroyed thyself." It is not God who condemns. "He that believeth not is condemned already." Punishment is the consequence of sin, not the sentence of the Father. "Thou hast destroyed thyself," said the Lord, "but——" thank God for that little word, that bids the soul turn from the dismal picture of sin, and look upon a picture of love and hope—"but in me is thine help."

The pit of sin is steep and deep. Help can come only from above, and wondrous help has come. God so loved that he gave his Son. Jesus stooped to the cross, that he might reach the lowest and the basest and save from the uttermost depths to the uttermost heights.

If there is joy in the presence of the angels over one sinner that repenteth, surely there is infinite joy in the Father's heart over every prodigal who returns to him.

The saved soul glorifies his name. If it means so much to the human soul to be rescued, what must it mean to the divine love to save! Deliverance and cleansing are therefore the pathway of God's glory. The whole Christian life is thenceforth for his name's sake. Let us never forget that we are saved not simply for ourselves, for our comfort or welfare, but that God might be glorified.

The glory of this salvation is that we are God's property, illumined by the spirit of Christ, and extending the kingdom of heaven upon this earth. The Name of names is written in our hearts, and upon our lives. "A little deeper, and you will find the emperor," said a wounded French soldier to the physicians operating upon him. So throughout our entire beings the glory of God's salvation will permeate until body, soul, and spirit complete the willing sacrifice. Let us be careful how we hold the Name before the world. Sin stains our own names, but salvation crowns us with his name of glory. We are not our own. We are Christ-men and Christ-women, living his life, and manifesting his holiness.

Soul of mine, thou hast felt the sting of sin in thy life. Hast thou also felt the touch of the scarred Hand of Calvary, that maketh all things whole? Hast thou entered into the fulness of the truth that thy salvation is a joy to the Father? Thou art forgiven not only that thou mightest have peace, but that thou also mightest glorify thy God.

Be watchful and faithful in thy sacred trusts. Take up thy tasks, small or great, with clean hands and a pure heart. Turn thy face toward the light, and thy darkness shall disappear, even as the night hastens away before the sunrise. Thy name is nothing. His name is all and in all, most sweet, most precious. Come daily for healing, for cleansing; for thou art not yet perfect, and one day, when he shall appear in glory and power, thou shalt be like thy blessed Saviour, for thou shalt see him as he is, to whom, together with the Father and the Holy Spirit, be power and honor and glory now and forevermore.

The Surrender.

Yield yourselves unto God, as those that are alive from
the dead.—*Rom.* 6 : 13.

THE Christian life is a life of self-sur-
render, by which we willingly and
trustfully yield our wills in order
that we might do God's will.
Reason clearly sides with revelation on this
point. Since our thoughts are not God's
thoughts, and he is perfect in wisdom and
knowledge, while we are ignorant and limited, we need God. The child for its own
good must yield itself to the superior wisdom of the parent or teacher, that it might
acquire knowledge and training. "Ap-
prenticeship alone leads to mastership."
We of older years have never really ceased
from attending school, and we learn in proportion as we yield our ignorance to the
wiser powers of others. How infinitely
truer this is in our spiritual life ! Not inde-
pendence, but sheer dependence, is our only
hope. Christ said, "Without me ye can
do nothing." Neither can we be anything.

Not all the intensest forms nor the most
vehement profession can induce spiritual
possession or power.   The secret of power
is absolute yielding to God, as a child yields
to the father, as a soldier simply obeys his
general.

> " Ours not to make reply,
>   Ours not to reason why,
>   Ours but to do and die,—"

or live, wherever God's voice summons us
to serve.

Not a single power of the mind or heart is
effaced by such yielding.   Nay, rather, we
only come to our true selves when God
dwells in us, and we have offered to him
our whole beings, in which he may will and
do of his good pleasure.

The branch that yields itself to the vine,
that through it the life of the vine may flow
to the outermost edge of leaf and twig,
bears the rich clusters of fruit, because it
abides in the vine, and yields itself to the
life of the vine.   " I am the vine, ye are the
branches," said Christ.

Sin is separation from God, a turning
away from him, and the soul seeks to reign
over its own little realm.   The mistakes and

failures in life come from the effort to have
our own way, to determine our own stand-
ards, to use our own strength, to rule ourselves. " Ye are not your own. Ye were
bought with a price." Yielding to God is
the fundamental principle of salvation. God
can save only a man who chooses to be
saved. Christ's lament over the Holy City
is most pathetic, because the occasion for it
is reproduced time and time again. " How
often would I have gathered thy children
together . . . and ye would not."

Yielding is also the essential element of
Christian service. We are not masters, but
disciples. We are "servants of the Most
High." "Yield yourselves unto God" by
a conscious choice. The margin gives a
striking version,— "Yield your members
as arms or weapons unto God."

We sing the hymn so often,—

> " Nearer, my God, to thee,
> Nearer to thee."

Let us translate that thought into a constant fact. Put yourself so close to the
hand of God that he can use you wherever
and whenever he wills. Let your members
be always God's weapons, which he may

use in his plans. Offer him clean hands, a pure heart, willing feet, consecrated lips, a holy life, and put all of these by a conscious choice near him. God can do anything with us and for us if we lie close to his hand of omnipotence. George Neumark uttered a great truth when, speaking of his hymns, he said, "I was only the instrument ; God swept the keys." The Father can do little for us if he can do little with us. He will add his deepest blessing as he uses the yielded life. Thus we may sing with Horatius Bonar :—

" Make use of me, my God,
    Let me not be forgot,
A broken vessel, cast aside,
    One whom thou needest not.

" All things do serve thee here,
    All creatures, great and small :
Make use of me, of me, my God,
    The weakest of them all."

MUCH MORE.

Much more, they which receive abundance of grace and of the gift of righteousness shall reign in life, by one, Jesus Christ.—*Rom.* 5 : 17.

PAUL undoubtedly caught the keynote of this message from the Master, who said, "I am come that they might have life, and that they might have it more abundantly."

Two small words gather up the thought, "much more." The apostle used this phrase five times in this chapter, to indicate the great contrast between the life under sin and the life under grace.

Sin has laid a heavy burden upon the soul. No wonder the spent life dismally sighs out the question, "Is life worth living?" Whose fault is it? The wilful human heart snapped the golden link which bound life to God. Made to live with him, it chose to wander from him. "The soul that sinneth, it shall die." Sin is powerful, but God's grace is much more powerful.

A lapidary purchased a very beautiful

29

stone, which was marred by a small crack.
The finder thought that this defect destroyed
the value of the jewel. But the artist cut
out the defect in making his design for a
signet-ring. "So God obliterates the conscience of sin by transforming it into the
consciousness of forgiveness. The cross
of Christ sinks deeper than the sense of
guilt." Life kills death. We are saved
from sin, that we might live the abounding
life.

Again, there is always much more for us
in our weakness. As princes of the royal
house, we have an inexhaustible storehouse
upon which we may draw. "My God shall
supply all your need according to his riches
in glory by Christ Jesus." There is always
more for us than we use, and we need
never grow anxious because conditions
seem to demand greater supplies of grace.
They which receive take out of the full and
exhaustless hand of God. Blessed are they
who hunger and thirst, for they shall not
only be filled, but they shall be made strong
enough to reign.

The regnant life is Christ's conquest of
us applied to our circumstances. "Be
strong in the Lord, and in the power of his

might." Dependence is the secret of our liberty and our strength. Our moral courage is God's life surging through willing channels in us. Our strength in prayer is conscious fellowship with the Saviour. Our abundance of faith is the Holy Spirit witnessing within us concerning Jesus.

The regnant life is an increasingly obedient life. Disobedience opposes our plans to God's. When our way crosses God's, then come the crosses; for the Father seeks to draw us back to his side. The assurance of victory is to let God have his perfect way. "This is the victory that overcometh the world, even our faith." We can win regnancy, not because we are strong, but because we have put our whole beings into the hands of our great Captain, who wins the battles for us, and then hands over the victory to us.

My soul, hast thou put on the whole armor of God ? Then fightings within and fears without can have no terrors for thee.

Art thou reigning, or art thou cast down because of defeat ? Art thou living at a poor dying rate, or the much more regnant life ? It is for thee to say. The Lord has offered thee the life more abounding. He has said that thou mayest reign if **thou wilt** receive.

What dost thou need to-day? More courage, more patience, more gentleness, more love? Behold, the Father's storehouse is open before thee. Ask in faith, and thou canst take. The Master will not withhold from thee if thou art willing to receive.

Dost thou need endurance? Why art thou so often defeated? Because thou art fighting alone. Art thou pressing forward, or art thou loitering in the rear? Be valiant and courageous. Through Christ alone canst thou conquer. With Christ alone art thou safe. In Christ alone canst thou reign.

THE THREE CROSSES.

God forbid that I should glory, save in the cross of our Lord Jesus Christ, by whom the world is crucified unto me, and I unto the world.—*Gal.* 6 : 14.

PAUL'S one great absorbing passion was Jesus, the crucified. He could have boasted of birth, of attainments and education; but all things were of little weight since the experience of the Damascus road held before him the vision of Christ. He knew one thing well. He knew whom he believed. His life was fixed upon the sacrifice of Calvary. As the traveller gazes upon the Mount of the Holy Cross, in our West land, until nature's silent witness to the tragedy of Golgotha becomes photographed upon the mental vision, never to be forgotten, so Calvary stood before Paul, a constant vision and inspiration, so that he could sing: "I glory in the cross of Christ. I am not ashamed to throw myself at its foot, and plead for mercy; for he who hung upon its crimsoned arms is my Lord and **Sav-iour.**"

1. The cross of the Lord Jesus Christ. We cannot fathom the mystery of godliness. Only this we do know: It was love, wondrous love, that sent Jesus to his cross. Sin made the cross necessary. Love accepted the necessity for a sacrifice. Now we can come to God by the way of the cross.

Princess Alice came into the room where her child was dying of a dread disease. "Mamma, kiss me." Prudence suggested a denial of the request. But mother-love stooped down and kissed the blackened lips. It meant death to the mother, but it also meant supreme love. Does God love any less? Nay, the Son stooped down from glory, bared his heart for the spear-thrust, stretched out his hands for the nails, that sinners might be loved back to the Father's heart.

His cross, planted in the earth, means that heaven has touched earth forever. Reaching up into the skies, it means that he will lead man to heaven. Stretching out with its wide arms, it means that the whole world may find a shelter in its embrace.

" Through all depths of sin and loss
    Sinks the plummet of the cross.
    Never yet abyss was found
    Deeper than that cross could sound."

2. "By whom the world is crucified unto me." Out of Christ's crucifixion grows the second cross. Can we say that with Paul? Jesus has put the world where it belongs—beneath his feet. He drew his motives from above. His mission upon earth was to glorify the Father.

This must be the motive of the saved soul. The world cannot furnish us with inspiration or with aims. It cannot suggest our joys or shape our living.

Christ came to save us from this present world. "I pray not that thou shouldest take them out of the world, but that thou shouldest keep them from the evil," from the fire of sin. The world, as God sees it, teems with base, ignoble purposes, and is at enmity with him. In Christ the world is crucified to the Christ-man; its mastery is broken. As we stand in the shadow of Calvary's cross, we read the definition of the world; and we say: "I will no longer live for the world, but for Christ. He is all the world to me."

3. "I am crucified unto the world." Paul chose the ignominy of the cross in preference to all that the world could offer. He willingly gave up all things for the excellency of the gospel. He did not wistfully look back and sigh for the old life because of the hardships of the present one. He chose to be a comrade with Jesus, of the despised cross, and that choice was final. Henceforth he bore the marks of the sufferings of Jesus.

A Christian had this dream: He seemed to be dead; and the angels, bending over him, said, "He is dead." They felt his heart, and whispered, "It does not throb." At last one came, and, lifting his hand, said: "Nay, what is this? A nail-print in his palm. This man is not dead; he has been crucified with Christ, and lives with him."

Blessed Father, we thank thee for the gift of thy love, thy dear Son, our Saviour. Give us grace, that not only the angels but the world may see that we live with Jesus a new life divine. Accept anew the glad dedication of body, soul, and spirit, that we may be true comrades of the cross, with Jesus Christ, our Saviour.

THE DIVINE PARTNERSHIP.

If ye shall ask anything in my name, I will do.—
John 14: 14.

OUR Saviour's farewell words to his disciples were meant to be sunbeams, lifting the mists of a dark summer foreboding.

A cloud of trouble was rising before them; but, "Let not your heart be troubled," the Master said. "I am going away, and yet not from you. I will not only prepare a place for you, but I will be with you alway. You may not understand all this now, but afterward you will know." The old promise was again about to be fulfilled, "Weeping may endure in the evening, but singing cometh in the morning."

Tenderly and lovingly the Saviour sought to draw his disciples away from the contemplation of parting into the blessed truth of spiritual fellowship.

The Christian need never be alone. Jesus has promised, "I am with you alway." In his utter solitude, when even the world may

37

forsake, the disciple may be sure that the heavenly Father will never leave or forsake his child. The dying Wesley said, with almost his last breath, "The best of all is, God is with us."

When Samuel Rutherford was in the Aberdeen prison, he wrote thus to a friend: "The Lord is with me; I care not what man can do. I burden no man, and I want nothing. No person is provided for better than I am. My chains are even gilded with gold. No pen, no words, nothing, can express the beauty of Christ. Every stone in my cell shines like rubies, because he is with me."

But Christ is not only with us; he is also working with us. What an omnipotent promise! "If ye shall ask anything in my name, I will do." Mark the fact that the little word, "it," found in the Authorized Version, is not in the original. The promise simply stands, "I will do." Jesus is the Doer. We are the petitioners. The union of Master and disciples constitutes the divine partnership. "If ye shall ask anything, in my name, I will be the Doer, I will be the answer to your prayers. I will see to it that all things work together for the good of my disciples." What an incentive this promise is, to work and pray as we have never done before!

What makes us more than conquerors, but this? Our great Captain obtains the victory for us, and then hands the triumph over to us. What does the promise mean, "Without me ye can do nothing," but this? Our weakness is linked with God's almightiness. The blessing of fellowship is involved in the divine partnership. We are God's workmanship, but we are also workers together with him. Thus the promise of the New Testament clasps hands with that of the Old, "Commit thy way unto me, and I will bring it to pass."

My soul, hast thou heard? dost thou believe? Hast thou been misled by that little word, "it," into thinking that the Father will only answer thy little requests, and will help thee only in the small things of thy pilgrimage? God can do all things. Do not limit the Father's love or power. Spend the promises lavishly. Bring large petitions, for thou art asking favors of the King of kings.

Wilt thou be made whole, that thou mayest do better service? He will cleanse thee until thy heart is washed whiter than snow, and he will heal thee until thy strength is wholly his; and then he can use thee. Wilt thou have victory over temptations, over a quick temper, over an overbearing passion, over a hot impatience? Ask him for his partnership, and he will do. His grace is always sufficient, if thou wilt only let him do with thee and for thee all that he desires.

First let God work in thee to will and to do of his good pleasure, and then he will lift thee into the exalted place of working with him; and thou wilt realize more and more the great joy of the divine fellowship in service.

GUIDANCE AND GLORY.

Thou shalt guide me with thy counsel, and afterward receive me to glory.—*Ps.* 73 : 24.

THE initial need of the human soul is sheer recovery from the penalty and the power of sin. Not by the power of the mind, nor by the might of the will, can man release himself from the thraldom of sin. God, infinite in mercy and love, has provided a release through the merits of his Son, upon whose innocent shoulders the storm spent itself, so that the soul might have a hiding-place from the winds and a covert from the tempest. After cleansing comes counsel, for the same Lord who said, "I am the Lord that healeth thee," also said, "I will guide thee." Faith sees the Saviour. Trust follows the Shepherd.

Daily must we come to him for counsel. Let us say, the first thing in the morning: "Blessed Lord, undertake for me. I do not know what is before me, but I know that thou art my Guide. Lead me, lest I stray away."

What an invincible Guide we have! An Alpine guide led a tourist party up the steep mountain, and came to a difficult pass. He steadied them, one by one, past the danger, holding out his hand as a support. One trembled as he faced the danger. The guide replied: "Do not fear. Only lean upon me. This hand never lost a traveller." Ah, that greater Hand held out in blessing to humanity, at last scarred on Calvary, never lost a soul intrusted to him. No power can pluck the soul out of his hand.

How do we receive his counsel? By prayer we commune with God. By our study of his Word he speaks to us. The Spirit enlightens the conscience and interprets the message. Religion is not an endless search after the truth. Here, in the Word, is the record of God's truth. Jesus said, "The Spirit will guide you into all truth." Accept the message. Study and dig deep. Compare duty with its commands. Square the life with the law. Match the work of the soul with the word of the Saviour. As the pillar of cloud by day and of fire by night guided the children of Israel through the wilderness, so the child of God is daily guided by the divine counsel.

And what then? So intimate and close becomes the relation between the Guide and the guided that the pathway of glory shines out, and brightens the whole outlook of the soul. The pilgrim can sing: "I am continually with thee; thou hast holden me by my right hand. Thou shalt guide me with thy counsel, and afterward receive me to glory." First comes training, then glory; first the work of discipline, then the finished journey; first the cutting of the jewel, then the sparkling of the gem; first the climbing, then the goal.

Christ's way, often rugged and thorn-strewn and difficult, always leads to the shining city of the skies. We cannot lose our way if we are with him; for he has said, "I am the way." Pilgrims travelling heavenward have their faces toward the light. Yonder at the pearly gates stands One ready to receive us, to welcome us, to make us feel at home, to say to us: "Thou didst have some dark days, but this glory was awaiting thee. Thy earthly pathway was ofttimes shadowed by cloud and torm. Now all trial is past. Here is neither sickness nor sorrow nor night nor tears. Enter, my child, into the glory and the joy of thy Lord."

Afterward! We do not know all now,
but ye "shall know hereafter." Afterward!
Heaven's great surprise will be a perfect explanation. Afterward ! We shall know
even as also we are known. Afterward!
It will be well with the soul. Afterward!
We may not know all the way now; but
we know our Guide, and then "we shall
be like him, for we shall see him as he is."
O tired soul, burdened with grief and trial,
shadowed by sorrow, and perplexed by
many unexplained chastenings, trust thy
Father God for the now and the afterward.

"God is his own interpreter,
And he will make it plain."

LOVE'S RESCUE.

Behold, on my peace came great bitterness, but thou hast loved my soul from the pit of corruption.—*Isa.* 38: 17. (Margin.)

HOW graphic and vivid a picture of the soul's rescue from the thraldom of sin! Two things came to the soul; the pain of bitterness, and the blessing of rescue. The first is the result of sin; the second is the work of love.

Man longs for peace, and never willingly gives up the thought of securing it. Though the world's false apples turn to ashes, yet the heart hopes. Sin is a heedless guide. It first digs a pit, and then leads the soul into the snare. It promises happiness, but gives bitterness. It whispers, "Your heart will be happy." It means, "Your heart will be bitter." It smiles the soul onward, and then gloats over its poor victim, a prisoner in the deep pit. It breaks the heart, and then chains it to the staple of despair in the prison-house of gloom.

What then? The soul has no power of

its own to scale the walls, or to break the
chains. What a mockery to say, "What
cannot be cured must be endured"!
What a crime to say, "Make yourself as
comfortable as possible, and by and by you
will develop out of this dreadful condi-
tion"! Nay ; "when lust hath conceived, it
bringeth forth sin ; and sin, when it is finished, bringeth forth death." This is the
evolution of sin. Is there no hope, no help?
Thank God for the supremacy of love. The
only help can come from above. The poor
prisoner of Chillon cut grooves in the slimy
walls, that he might get a little nearer to the
light ; but he could not escape. Thank God
for the blessed word of hope. "Behold, I
have anointed my Son to bind up the
broken-hearted, to proclaim liberty to the
captives, and the opening of the prison to
them that are bound." Jesus came to save
from the uttermost to the uttermost. He
stands at the opening of the pit. His very
presence brings light and hope. Already
there is a strange stirring of the heart as it
looks up and sees love. The Master has
come, whose very face inspires confidence.
As he looks into the face of the prisoner, he
says, "I am able and willing to save thee ;

art thou willing that I should?" Only believe, poor sinner; for he has come to lift up thy despairing heart and to save thee.

There is always a strange shrinking of sin before the presence of Christ, just as darkness gathers up its robes of gloom and departs when the glory-beams of the sun climb up the golden stairway of the morning dawn. The stifling atmosphere clears, and even the pit, boasting so often of its power, now feels that it is face to face with its Master.

Power linked itself with love, might and mercy joined hands, when Jesus stood at the tomb of Lazarus, his friend. Love cried out, through a rainbow of tears, "Lazarus, come forth." The tomb felt the power of the Conqueror, and even death knew its Lord.

So love stands at the dark pit of sin, and lifts the willing soul out of its lowest depths, shatters the chains that bind hand and foot, breaks the spell that binds the heart, and exclaims, "Now thou art free." Blessed Saviour, thou hast loved my soul out of the pit. Thy love has conquered. Thou hast led me from darkness into the light, from despair into hope, from weakness into strength, from death unto life, from the thraldom of Satan into the kingdom of thy love.

What shall I do now? Shall I continue in sin, that grace may abound? Shall my life be a constant falling and rescue? God forbid. I lived unto sin once; now help me to live wholly unto thee. O, 't was love, 't was wondrous love, that saved me, and every fibre of my being thrills with gratitude unto thee. May I never wander from the spell of thy love over me. Thou hast freed me; give me grace to use this freedom wholly for thee, in thy service, going out and coming in, as the bond-servant of thy love." My soul, lift up thy hymn of praise to thy Redeemer.

He brought me up also out of an horrible pit,
Out of the miry clay.
He set my feet upon a rock,
And established my goings.
He hath put a new song in my mouth,
Even praise unto our God.

—Ps. 40; 2, 3.

THE VISION OF GOD.

This is none other but the house of God, and this is the gate of heaven.—Gen. 28: 17.

THE religious nature is the deepest element in life, but that element may lie neglected in the human soul. Jacob of old is the striking example of this thought. Destined for a high place in the plans of God, he sought to gain this supremacy by deceitful methods, and thus his plans were turned into defeat. In his extremity the Lord appeared to him in the lonely solitude of the plains, and aroused in him the capacity to see the divine. The background was his own failure and his exile. With a stone as his pillow, the open heavens as his covering, he lay down in utter helplessness and despair. Then the heavens opened to him so that he saw somewhat of the glory, and he beheld the descending and the ascending angels. The soul, far removed from the deceits of the world, conscious of its own failure, faced heavenward, and thought on God.

49

No wonder that Jacob upon awaking felt the power of God stirring within him. He had seen something of God. The aspect of his life from henceforth would in some measure be changed. After that vision he could not be the same man as before.

Mark the fact that the place had not changed. The same silence reigned. The same barren stretch of plain extended before him. The same bowlders lay at his feet. The stone pillow had not been transformed into jasper or pearl, but he had changed. He had seen the vision of the divine. Heaven had opened to him, with all its pure and uplifting influences; the consciousness of God's presence had penetrated his inmost soul. This was the real beginning of that transformation which changed Jacob into Israel as a prince who had prevailed with God. That is the deep lesson for us. True religion means more than interest in history, or the mastery of ethics and moral philosophy. We need a meeting-place where the soul can stand face to face with God and receive from him the vision of what life means, of the forces of life that strengthen the soul, of the power that links the possibilities of life with the armies and the chariots of heaven.

Our souls need such experience as Jacob
had, to clarify our vision of eternity, and to
make them conscious of God's presence.
Prayer is much more than speaking words.
It is the soul breathing the very life of God.
It is joining the deepest reality of the spiritual life with the common, every-day duties
of living. The soul would be at a serious
loss if it only had an abstract principle upon
which to base the exercise of prayer. God's
Word frequently connects prayer with a
place. Jesus associated prayer with place
when he sought the solitude of the mountain or the deep shades of an olive grove in
order to be removed from the noises of the
world and to enter into the solemn hush of
the Father's presence. How earnestly he
urged upon the disciples the need of enter-
ing into the closet, "and when thou hast
shut thy door, pray to thy Father which is
in secret." Did not Jesus mean that we
were to have a place in our lives which
should be filled with the most sacred associ-
ations, and be surrounded by holy influences
and hallowed experiences?

My soul, hast thou a holy of holies in the
daily life; a place where thou canst retire,
and meet thy Father God, and commune

with him ? Thou dost enter into the spirit
of public worship and prayer; canst thou
also rejoice in the presence of God when
thou art alone with him ? Canst thou hold
thyself still enough so that the world is far
removed, and thou dost not wander in
thought or grow weary in waiting ? Dost
thou give only a few hurried moments in
the morning, or a few wearied moments in
the evening, for such a privilege of meeting
with thy Father ? How canst thou work
well if thou dost pray so poorly ? Remember that the disciples of old went from the
upper room to the harvest of souls. O, seek
often thy closet, and open wide thy door,
that the heavenly Guest may enter; and then
shut thy door to all the world, and verily
thou shalt see God, and thou canst then live
the transfigured life of thy Lord.

THROUGH KNOWLEDGE TO TRUST.

They that know thy name will put their trust in thee.
—*Ps.* 9: 10.

HOLY Spirit, teach us a deeper lesson concerning this simple, every-day privilege of trust. Help us to fill our empty chalices at the fountain of eternal waters, that our souls' thirst might be quenched.

Faith is more than the apprehension of a doctrinal truth. Its truest expression is love for a person. We may say reverently that God always respects the powers of the mind and the heart with which he has endowed us. Jesus asked his disciples to believe the message which he brought, because confidence in and love for him had been awakened.

We so often speak of the basis of faith. What is the nature of that basis? We are continually demanding proof when we really need knowledge. Think for a moment of earthly relations. Faith rests much more on our confidence in trustworthy men than on sheer evidence which we receive through the senses. We know the man, and we then trust his word. Life grasps life by coming to know and to love it. They that know will trust. We rejoice in the precious message that God knows us. "The Lord knoweth them that are his." We rejoice in his perfect knowledge of us. "The good shepherd giveth his life for the sheep." "I know my sheep."

But this is the other side of the truth. They who learn to know God will come to trust him, and the more they know him, the more will they trust. But mark this distinction between two kinds of knowledge. The one demands a perfect explanation before it can accept a message; the other asks for a closer fellowship with the one who reveals the message. The one wants proof; the other seeks love. Science is what we know by proof; religion is what we accept through confidence in God.

What folly it is to hold God at arm's length, and say, "I will not come closer until I know thee better"! In our friendships do we say: "I should like to have more confidence in you, and trust you more; but I must hold aloof from you until

I find you trustworthy"? We associate with friends, and live with them; and, as we learn to know them, we also learn to trust them. Without fellowship, trust such as God expects cannot exist. You might as well try to compel a little child to follow a total stranger as to make your heart trust God without living with him and loving him.

"Faith cometh by knowledge," by hearing God's Word, the hearing of obedience. "He that hath my commandments, and keepeth them, he it is that loveth me." "Religion is the response of the inner to the outer." It is the human heart answering its divine Lord. Come to the Word with a candid mind, a receptive soul, a willing heart, saying, "Dear Lord, reveal thy Word to me, and manifest thyself through thy Word." The Bible interprets God; but much more, God will interpret the Bible to us.

Through knowledge to trust was the shining pathway which St. Paul trod with so much joy and triumph. Not even the darkness and the gloom of the Mamertine prison could shake his deep faith, for we can hear the triumph of victory in his very words, "I know whom I have believed, and am persuaded that he is able to keep that which I have committed unto him against that day."

Blessed Father, forgive me for being so slow to learn the privilege of trust. Thou hast revealed thyself through thy Son, that I might know thee, and that, knowing thee, I might implicitly trust thee.

Give me the still hour, the quiet heart, that I may be conscious of thy presence. Calm the turbulency of my anxious heart with thy gentle grace. Dispel my misgivings by revealing thy Word to me. Help me to study the Bible with the calm consciousness that thou art speaking to me through it. Thou knowest the trials of my faith. Forgive me if I walk slowly, for I am as a little child before thee. Thou art my Lord. I will trust thee. I will obey thee. Sanctify the time allotted to me for my earthly life so that I may live wholly for thy glory and love.

The Higher Life.

Seek the Lord, and ye shall live.—*Amos* 5 : 6.

HERE is life and life. The evidence of physical existence is our breath and our activity. We live and move and have our being, because God is our Creator. In the beginning God—. We live because he lives and wills and loves.

But there is a higher life, which controls and shapes the physical, and manifests the image of God in us, though that image has been blurred and stained by the sins of our hearts.

The command to seek the Lord presupposes the power to seek, to think, to love. The dead cannot see. The lifeless cannot seek. God founds the possibility of seeking him upon the powers that he himself has given to man. We must have belonged somewhere if ever we were lost; and salvation means that the Son of God brings us back again to the Father to whose heart and home we originally belonged, and from which we wandered. Seek, and ye shall find. There is no mystery; for, as we open the heart, God will come in with the wealth of his love and his life.

God is love, and we shall find love in him. God is mercy, and he enters the human heart, and makes us conscious of forgiveness because of the sacrifice on Calvary. God is truth, and the Holy Spirit abides at the centre of our being to testify of Jesus.

We seek God, but infinitely more God seeks us, that he may live in us and rule and reign over us. That is the higher life. Faith apprehends and trust appropriates. Love finds. A man has not truly begun to live until Christ lives in him. Paul said, "To me to live is Christ." He had made the supreme search and the supreme surrender. "I live; yet not I, but Christ liveth in me."

The child born blind lived, but could not see. When in after years sight was restored, she saw beauty all around, and she exclaimed: "How beautiful! Mother, why did you not tell me how lovely everything was?"

"My child, I tried to tell you, but you could not understand it."

"Ye must be born again," is the message which leads to the true life. We cannot see, we cannot live as God counts life, unless we have sought and found God, by the obedience of our faith and our acceptance of Jesus as the Lamb slain for us.

Seek the Lord, not merely to know something about him, not to be interested in his providences; but seek him for his sake, with an energy of trust, until you have passed the borders of the promised land and are in his presence. Then comes the true life, the life more abounding.

"Thou shalt live." That surely does not mean that these bodies will go on breathing; for we see all around us men who refuse to seek the Lord, who are indifferent to every plea of love and offer of mercy; yet they live. But eternity determines the character of life. God means that the soul, seeking and finding him, shall know the power of an endless life, and shall not come into condemnation, but shall, now and forever, pass from death unto life.

My soul, hast thou heard? "Seek the Lord, and thou shalt live." Thy very life is at stake. Thou mayest be dying before thy body decays. Thou art meant for a nobler purpose than simply to breathe. God's life is held out to thee. Seek that first. Thou wilt have no rest until thou findest thy rest in him. Dost thou thirst for the living God? Thank God that thou art thirsty, for then thou wilt seek the eternal fountain, and drink. Art thou hungry? Thank God, for then thou wilt press into the banquet of love, and thou wilt be satisfied, and wilt receive of his fulness.

Thou shalt truly live only as thou art bound up in the bundle of life with thy Lord. In the secret of his presence, like Moses of old, thou mayest lift up thy weak hand, and, laying it in the hand of Omnipotence, thou wilt feel the thrill of the eternal life within thee; and thou canst sing in the very hour of dying and in the presence of death: "I live, I live forever. Thanks be unto God, who giveth me the victory through my Lord and Saviour, Jesus Christ."

The Stimulus of Defeat.

As for thee, the Lord thy God hath not suffered thee so to do.—*Deut.* 18 : 14.

THERE are certain providences of God with which we are not so familiar because we are not always sure that they are blessings, although faith ought to accept God's Word implicitly. Mercies in disguise are not very popular with us, because we cannot clearly see whether they are friend or foe, nor can we always make out their meaning.

Is there any comfort in the thought that it is much better for us in many instances not to have certain things ? Next to getting, contentment is the cheerful willingness to do without many things. This experience is so often beyond our understanding that it makes us unhappy and discontented.

God's wisdom, which wrought so lovingly for the children of Israel, is still at work among those who put their trust in him. God leads, and he withholds. The Lord provides, and he denies. The Lord has suffered us to do, and then he has not suffered us to do. We thank God for giving. Shall we not also thank him for not giving? If we only knew all, if we could only enter into all the complicated needs of character-building, and what it means to guard human life, we could then understand why God finds it necessary to withhold as well as to give, since his thoughts are not our thoughts, nor are his ways our ways.

If the thin veil of the material could be drawn aside, we might mark the dangers that pressed so near us, and threatened us with dire peril ; but the hand omnipotent was stretched out in our defence, and the danger was thrust aside, and we never knew of it at all. In many ways unknown to us, God's providences are alert sentinels for our safety. We shield our children from harm and danger by interfering with their desires. The child does not know ; the parent does ; and therefore the child's ignorance is protected by the parent's knowledge. The Heavenly Father will not permit us to enter upon what his supreme wisdom knows will injure us or mar our souls.

Have we not found another reason why

the law of the Kingdom is, Not our wills,
but God's will, be done ? We do not know
very much. We are limited on all sides.
But God knows and understands. Let him
have his perfect way. Jesus in his earthly
ministry set himself to the serious task of
moulding common material into serious discipleship. He gave his followers much,
but he also denied them much. The Master
Moulder works upon the characters of his
disciples of all ages. "What I do thou
knowest not now, but thou shalt know
hereafter." It is not necessary to know the
whole process ; it is sufficient to know that
we are safe in his blessed hands. There is
stimulus in defeat when trust can say, in
the face of some denial, "Thou knowest
best." If the Father withholds, we can be
sure that he has something better to give.
If he takes away, we can be sure that it will
work for our good. Let his providence
spur us on to deeper faithfulness.

An agonizing father knelt at the bedside
of his only son, who was dying.

"I cannot give you up, my son."

The child replied, "Papa, find some other
boys to take care of and to help."

A university founded and endowed by

the parents, where needy boys might receive an education, was the result of the death of an only son, who in dying gave a new life-motto to his parents.

May we read many messages concerning our life-work in the mellow or shaded light of our losses and our defeats. Let us patiently set our hearts to the most difficult tasks, because the Lord, who gives and withholds, always knows what we need ; and, though we may not now be able to fathom the plans of divine providence in our lives, or find a present key for each mystery, let us trust God, and be willing, obedient children, content to believe that he doeth all things well.

" And, when through patient toil we reach the land
 Where tired feet with sandals loose may rest,
When we shall clearly see and understand,
 I think that we will say, ' God knew the best.' "

PAUL'S THREE AMBITIONS.

For me to live is Christ.—Phil. 1 : 21.

THE whole life of the great apostle was intensified by this one thought, that Christ might reign supreme in him, and that the spirit of Christ might freely work through him.

Zinzendorf, the ardent missionary of the last century, manifested the same intense purpose, when he said, "I have only one passion; that is he, only he."

It is wrong not to be ambitious when such ambition means that the life is wholly given over to the life divine to do with it as God pleases. Dr. A. J. Gordon, of sainted memory, called special attention to the following three ambitions, which throbbed in Paul's consecrated life.

1. "Be ambitious to be quiet." 1 Thess. 4: 11. Its primary reference was to a very practical duty, but its application to the spiritual life is obvious. "In quietness is your strength." Fellowship with God can be conserved only as our souls are still

enough before him so that we can hear his voice and be conscious of his presence. We are prone to live noisy lives. We are fond of activity and outward striving. We often mistake a stirring nature for deep living. The measure of our willingness to wait upon God will determine the measure of our spiritual strength. Deep lives are those that know the quietness of God's presence. "We come to the mercy-seat on an errand of real life." God will hear us if we will hear God. There is too much hurry in our lives, too little desire to be alone with God. We are fitted for our most arduous tasks only by being conscious of God's presence in our quiet moments. If we would know how to work more, let us learn how to pray better.

2.   "Wherefore we labor, that, whether present or absent, we may be accepted of him." 2 Cor. 5: 9.

Paul's great desire was to please God. He worked and toiled under the eye of the Father. He cared not what the world thought. He did care what God thought concerning his daily life. It is so hard for us to realize that God sees us. "Thou God seest me" in all the details of my living.

We are in this world, not to please it, but to please God. May we hate all sham and hypocrisy, and cease forever from being time-servers, and be out-and-out God-servers. Let us, in all places and at all times, be ambitious to please him.

3. " Yea, so have I strived to preach the gospel, not where Christ was named, lest I should build upon another man's foundation." Rom. 15: 20.

Next to Christ, Paul's great passion was for souls. He yearned to carry the gospel to those who had not heard the name of Jesus. He wanted to be the herald to the most forlorn hope, an under-shepherd, following his Master out on the bleak and barren mountain slopes, hunting lost sheep.

We are called to be workers for souls. Every member of Christ's church is a missionary, a pastor. Christ meant that when he said, " Go ye." The school of prayer, the quiet hour, the duty of pleasing him,— all this leads to the wholesome passion for souls.

It is a mistake to think that the church exists only for the comfort of its members. It is a sheepfold, with a great many straying sheep on the outside. " Bring them in," said Jesus. Out yonder, men and women are sinning, suffering, dying. Here are Christ's men and Christ's women, who have been rescued and are saved. If Christ were here, what would he do? He would first seek and save the lost. But Christ is here in the person of every disciple who has received the Spirit. He has also given his commission. "Go ye and disciple lost souls in my name. Live a pioneer life for me. Go forth to the conquest of souls for my sake. Lovest thou me, then feed my sheep. Make it your supreme passion to rescue human life at every life-saving station because of love for me. I am going to the uttermost parts of the earth. Whither go ye? Are you ambitious to go with me?"

What answer shall we give? O, there can be only one answer as Christ is transfigured before us, and we read our most sacred obligations in the light of his love and life. Yes,

"I 'll go where you want me to go, dear Lord,
    Over mountain or plain or sea;
I 'll say what you want me to say, dear Lord;
    I 'll be what you want me to be."

Love Seeking Love.

Lovest thou me more than these?—John 21 : 15.

THE Master met the defeated disciple, and forgave the denial by testing Peter's love. He does not say, "Peter, why didst thou deny me?" but, "Lovest thou me? Have repentance and sorrow clarified thy heart, until the dross has been swept away, and thou art conscious of thy love for me?" Peter was not ready to serve until he was ready to love. Has Christ ever met us along the shore of life's sea, and has he put the same question to us, "Tell me, dost thou really love me?" What answer have we given?

We are in danger of magnifying the tangible and the practical, and of losing sight of the heart-life, without which all service is vain and perfunctory. We often say with a sigh, "We must do this or that in our service for God." I wonder what the Father thinks of that word, "must." Compulsion stifles love. Cold duty is a heartless service. Christ's love constrains us,

69

but it will never compel us. Let us love God for his own sake. May we never grow so formal, so absorbed in our work, that we never say, "Dear Father, I love thee." The little child comes to its father, and stirs his heart by saying, "Dear papa, I just love you." Are we not the children of God, and has he not said, "I have loved thee with an everlasting love"?

An aged Scotch wife lay dying. The sorrowing husband sat at her side, and, seeing that she was soon to leave him, he broke through his lifelong reserve, and said, "Jane, if ever a woman was loved, I love you." The weary eyelids were raised, a radiant smile illumined her face, as she replied, "I kenned it, John, but O to hear you say it!"

How much we lose by not giving expression to our love! Why should we not often and often tell out our love to the one beloved? Why should we not be childlike enough to tell God of our love for him, and to answer his blessed love with our intense affection?

When the Master sought to teach the deepest lesson of the life of his kingdom, he placed a little child before the disciples.

No matter how many years crown our heads, the heart must remain childlike, if we would live with our Father God.

The great core and sweetness of Christly fellowship is the Master's question and Peter's answer. "Lovest thou me?" "Yea, Lord, thou knowest that I love thee." "But, Peter, lovest thou me more than thou lovest any one or anything else? Am I first in thy heart?" What is our answer?

The Psalmist's heartstrings thrilled with a pulse divine when he sang those words: "Whom have I in heaven but thee? and there is none on earth that I desire beside thee."

Love sends the loving heart out into the world to carry its message to other lives. That is the test of sincerity.

My soul, dost thou love much or little? Remember her of old of whom the Saviour said she loved much because much had been forgiven her. Hast thou met thy Lord in the way? Perhaps yesterday thou didst deny him. Shame upon thy weakness. Do not shun him. Stand face to face with him to-day. Listen; he is speaking to thee. "My child, lovest thou me?" Gather up all thy energy, thy power of faith and love, and let thy heart speak. Thrust the world aside, that thou mayest see only him. "Dost thou really love me?" Canst thou say: "Blessed Lord, thou knowest all things. Thou knowest that deep down in my heart love for thee reigns and abides. Help me to express it to thee, to live in thy great love for me." Listen for the next answer. "My child, the best way to show thy love for me is to love my other children enough to feed them and unselfishly serve them. Tell to others the story of thy Jesus and his love." Let this be the motto on thy shield, as thou dost go forth in the name of the King of love, "I love; therefore I serve."

THE FORGOTTEN PLACE.

My people . . . have forgotten their resting-place.—
Jer. 50 : 6.

OW often the Christian longs for rest, and then does not really seek for it! We sing about it, we pray for it, we meditate upon it, as a sort of poetical fancy, but we are slow to take this rest from the outstretched hand of God.

What is the true rest which God is so willing to give us ? It is surely not inaction. The most restless, joyless life is the indolent one. It cannot be a life of untroubled ease, for Jesus said that one of the marks of discipleship would be tribulation. It cannot be rest from burdens, or cessation from difficult service; for the rest of God can be appreciated only by those who actually bear the heat and the burden of the day. The invitation is to those who are weary and heavy laden. Those who are not will not care to come.

Not rest from, but rest amid, the tasks of life; the rest of weakness which feels behind it the strength of Omnipotence; the rest of faith, which knows God's sustaining grace,—this is the rest which the Father offers. Scientists tell us that rest is absolutely essential for the body, in order to supply the waste tissues, and to build up that which energy has used up. That law is just as true for the soul. We need spiritual strength daily. We have not an innate or latent supply. God alone is the reservoir of our power. We may build our own reservoirs, but they are only like those which Jeremiah saw, scarring the hill-slopes, "broken cisterns."

God knows our inmost and utmost need. He is our very present help. God is the home of the soul. He is the resting-place of the heart. His secret place is secure from all invasion. We may live outwardly in the midst of uncertainty and change, close by strain and stress; but the Lord changes not, and in his presence there is always serenity and peace. He will lift the life above every danger-point. The Lord is my fortress, the rock of my salvation. The eternal God is my refuge, and underneath are the everlasting arms.

But God has a warning word for us.

"My people have forgotten their resting-place." What poor memories we do have! We forget and forget, until we almost think that forgetting is a sufficient excuse. In God's sight it is a grievous sin to forget when it means lack of earnest faith and of thoughtful obedience.

We forget when the energy of the self-life seeks to usurp the mastery of the Christ-life. How often we ask for mercies, and are never long enough at the mercy-seat to receive them!

We forget our resting-place when the means become ends instead of pathways up to God. We forget when we resist the Holy Spirit, and follow our own desires. We are so engrossed in our duties that we lose the consciousness of God's presence. "In returning and rest shall ye be saved; in quietness and in confidence shall be your strength."

"My people have forgotten," not their market-place, but "their resting-place." What help is the fountain when we turn away and stoop to the pool? What blessings can the still waters bring if we are wholly in the turbulent streams of life? Come back to God as the heart's resting-

place.   Rest on the eternal foundations.
Steady the soul upon the Rock of Ages.
The hand clasped in God's omnipotent, loving hold will no longer grasp at mere earthly
things.   Everything will be sacred.   Everything will be God's.

O my soul, never forget thy resting-place,
forget not that thy place of power is also
thy place of rest; for, as thou dost serve,
thou mayest also lean upon the everlasting
arms.

Blessed Father, we need thy constant
presence.   We want to know thee better.
Give us wisdom to esteem above all else the
blessing of resting upon thee.   Thou wilt
forgive our sins, but thou dost never forget
us.   Forgive us for forgetting, and help us
to be more thoughtful, more responsive to
thy life and love.   Draw us closer to thy
strong and warm heart, so that we may
never forget that thou art the true home of
the soul.

Through the Fires.

For he is like a refiner's fire. And he shall sit as a refiner and purifier of silver.—*Mal.* 3: 2, 3.

THE Lord speaks to us in words which we can understand. The Lord is like—and then follows some human relation which pictures a daily scene or a common occurrence, translating his wise plans.

He is like a refiner, nay, like the refiner's fire itself, worker and implement combined. He will not leave the precious work of refining a human soul to circumstances or to abstract, soulless things. He works, he moulds, he refines. He comes with the fire. His hand holds the instrument. In his control are the fires which cleanse and purify.

How this precious truth lifts the whole thought of pain and sorrow and bitter experience out of the mystery of the unknown into the realm of the Father's doings and of our faith and trust!

We are the ore, holding within our sentient beings much that is precious and also much that is base and ignoble. The two cannot lie together and form godly character. Man has tried for ages to discover some human alchemy by which the heart might be purified and the soul washed of its sin. Centuries of ingenuity have been expended in the vain search. The world has been challenged to bring forth its subtlest plans, its wisest theories, its deepest philosophies. Who can forgive sin? What power can bring golden conduct out of leaden thought? All has been in vain, save as human life has listened to the words and the voice of God. ''Come and let us reason together,'' not about the fact of sin. That needs no argument. But this, God is willing to do, if we are willing that he shall do it for us: '' Though your sins be as scarlet, they shall be white as snow.''

The type and symbol of salvation found its perfect fulfilment in the cross, and upon that cross hung the bleeding Son of God, who for the joy that was set before him despised the shame, that he might save the souls of men. He passed through the fires, that we might be spared the bitterness of the ordeal; and, now that a perfect reconciliation has been made, he is ever seeking to crown human life with the glory of the Father. Jesus Christ is the refiner and the fire. He is the power and the wisdom of God, who cleanses the heart, and out of the poor, powerless material brings forth the spotless character and the shining soul. His fire of love burns out the dross and purifies the life.

This is certainly true in the sanctification of the soul. We have not as yet attained, nor are we yet perfect. Much needs yet to be done before we walk in white in the city beyond the skies. Jesus is seeking to put upon us the sterling stamp of perfect workmanship.

For this reason we pass through the refining fires of disappointments, which are really his appointments. Sorrow and pain come with their heavy burdens, not to crush us, but to take out of our lives the things that are useless and debasing. Let Jesus do his perfect work in us. He desires to see in us the divine image, for a refiner sits at his work, and is sure that the fire has burned out all the dross only when he can see his own image reflected in the molten mass. Until the Lord sees in us his re-

flected image the furnace experience must
be ours.

"Blessed are the pure in heart, for they
shall see God." Shall we shrink from the
ordeal when we know the divine purpose?
Shall the ore say, "Not now: I fear the
fire; I dread the pain"? Nay, welcome
the chastening which makes the divine image brighter in us. It may seem grievous
now, but "afterward it yieldeth the peaceable fruit of righteousness."

Welcome the wound which has such a
great Physician to heal it, who promises
perfect health. Welcome the discipline of
the one hand when with the other hand he
draws us closer to him. Welcome the fire
and the refiner's toil of love when the precious treasure of the Lord is separated from
all that tarnishes and debases, and the shining soul is the finished work.

"Who would not have pain like mine
To be consoled like me?"

GOD'S PROPERTY.

I have called thee by thy name; thou art mine.—*Isa.*
43: 1.

IT is very important for us to have
positive thoughts concerning God.
We ought to be familiar with his
Word, but much more we ought to
know God. Eliphaz said, "Acquaint now
thyself with him, and be at peace." To
know God brings peace. To be a stranger
to him means unrest and orphaned life,
and at last eternal separation.

The knowledge of God is the aim of the
Word. Jesus came to reveal the Father.
Paul cries out, "That I might know him."
And then, when the closing days came, he
exclaimed in triumph, "I know whom I
have believed." It is most blessed to know
God, for Jesus taught us to say, "Our
Father." We are his children, the mem-
bers of his family.

It is our privilege to realize what the
Father thinks of us, what he is willing to
do for his children. He knows us. He

loves us. He remembers our names. The
Good Shepherd said, "I know my sheep."
He calls them by name. He cares for them
and protects them.

As a child is reassured in the dark by a
father's voice, so we can hear the voice of
the Father bidding us, "Fear not, for I have
redeemed thee." Salvation is a family
blessing. As God's children, we are saved
from sin and temptation, and kept from
danger, all along life's journey. The
Father's roof over us, the Father's hand
grasping ours, the Father's love round about
us, as the mountains are round about Jeru-
salem,—this is the great privilege of the
Father's children.

How tender his love is in the speaking of
these words! "I have called thee by thy
name, thou art mine!" We bear the name
of Christ, and are known as Christ's men
and Christ's women. His name is our inspiration for service and our plea in prayer.
The native African convert, desiring to
work for his Lord, came to the missionary,
and said, "I am now a Jesus Christ man."

But mark the meaning of the message.
"I have called thee by *thy name*." Amid
all the numberless creations in the universe

God can single out his children and call them by name.

Imagine the thrill of joy when in a strange place and amid a multitude of foreign people we should hear our names mentioned, and recognize a familiar voice. What a blessed truth! The Father calls us by name. He whispers it to us amid our afflictions and trials. "I know you and love you." He speaks to us, when temptation surges in upon us. "I am watching over you."

"Now are we the sons of God." We belong to a family, the Father of which intimately knows all the children. Let us not be misled or deceived into thinking that God does not care for us in all the details of living or in the smallest affairs of our life. He knows, he loves, he cares. Take him at his word. Accept his promises, and then with eager love and faith spend them lavishly. Use these promises, as love's provision, for every emergency, and press them into their fullest meaning and purpose.

"The Master is come, and calleth for thee." As a father, by simply calling, can indicate his wishes to a child, so the Heavenly Father expects us to be in such close fellowship with him, faith so willing, conscience so sensitive, heart so pure, that we can respond and obey.

My soul, thy Lord calleth thee by name. Let not any worldly thing influence thee or dull thy ear so that thou canst not hear and answer. Remember whose thou art and whom thou servest. Be sensitive to God's voice. Live so near to the gate of heaven that its life may flood thy life, and stand so near to the Lord's throne that he may send thee instantly upon his errands. See to it that thy name is untarnished and unstained, that, when he desires to call thee, he may not find it impossible to speak thy name because it is impure and spotted.

May thy God put his seal of favor and delight upon thy life, so that the world may read this message, though it may not understand thy source of power: " This life belongs wholly to God."

The Divine Pattern.

See that thou make all things according to the pattern shewed to thee in the mount.—*Heb.* 8 : 5.

THE greatness of our God is revealed in his control of the details of life with the same concern and regard which he manifests in ruling the whole universe.

The first tabernacle, erected among the children of Israel, and standing for the presence and the worship of God, was not planned by Moses or any other earthly architect. Human ingenuity and wisdom were illumined from above. "Before Moses built it, he saw the whole plan and pattern of it, in prophetic vision. In some secluded spot, on Sinai's heights, the tabernacle stood before him, woven out of sunbeams; and then he descended to the mountain-foot to repeat the vision in actual curtains, gold, and wood."

God is in his holy temple, because he first designed it, and then as owner he occupies his rightful place.

"Know ye not that ye are the temple of the Holy Ghost?" We are the tabernacles of God, and he is ever seeking souls who will build temples according to his plan and purpose.

Jesus came to tell us what it meant to be a temple of the living God. He came to dwell with men, that he might teach men to dwell with God. His name is Emmanuel, "God with us," in order that he might reveal to us the supreme privilege of offering to the Father a dwelling-place.

What a radiant thought! God pleads with us to be spiritual builders, and to make all things according to the pattern of his Son, that he might come in and abide with us.

As means of grace this spiritual temple has three rooms. First, the Scripture-room. God has spoken to us in words that we may hear and understand. The Bible is his Word. We cannot build without consulting his plan. Search the Book. Study the Word. How can the Holy Spirit testify of Jesus to us if we have little knowledge of him?

Second, the throne-room. Christ must be the Lord of the life. The obedience of faith crowns him King of kings. He must be the sole owner of the soul. Each heart must have a coronation service in which Jesus becomes the all and in all. "I live, yet not I, but Christ liveth in me." I live, but Christ sits upon the throne, and reigns over me. Live in the throne-room, until you enter into the fulness of that word, "my Lord." Put Jesus on the throne, hand over everything to him, and let him reign and rule with the sceptre of his power.

Third, the holy of holies, the prayer-room. The purpose of temple-building is to glorify God, to witness for Christ. "There I will meet with thee, and I will commune with thee." The whole visible tabernacle was this centre, the mercy-seat, and everything else was built around it. The Christian who neglects to live in the prayer-room cannot hope to grow in grace. We cannot be true disciples and refuse to seek the mercy-seat.

Jesus was the great master of prayer. The quiet hour, alone with his Father, on the mountain-slope or beside the inland sea, meant everything to him.

When Moses finished all the preliminary work, the glory of the Lord came down and filled the temple by day and by night. As we live with God, and cease from all our human plans and human strivings, God's fulness will come in upon us, and his glory will be shed abroad in our hearts.

Are these three rooms our living-rooms in our Christian life, or have we closed them or neglected them, and are we living somewhere on the outside? The Word, the throne, the prayer, how much do they mean in our lives? May we truly say: "I cannot live my Christian life without abiding in these sanctuaries of the temple. They are my living-rooms." O Father, interpret thy word to me in the Scripture-room. O Saviour, reign entirely over me, in my throne-room, for thou art my King. O Sanctifier, lead me into the presence of my God, so that my prayer-room may open out before the divine mercy-seat.

THE TIME FACTOR.

Remember how short my time is.—*Ps.* 89 : 47.

SCIENCE or philosophy may explain something about life, but God alone can reveal its plan and destiny. We are in contact with the tangible, but we are also surrounded by the invisible. To-day is linked with the eternal. Mark the passing of time. David recalls the brevity of his allotted moments. Paul speaks of the fact, "Time is short." John in the beginning of Revelation points to the importance of his message, for "the time is at hand." In the progress of the vision the angel bears this solemn message, "Time no longer." Thus the history of the soul on this earth may be expressed in the terms of time. Even though we reach seventy years, fifteen years of childhood and twenty years of unconscious sleep take up half of it, and days of sickness and sorrow draw heavily upon the other half. What does our dower of time mean? God's Word speaks plainly. "Here you fix your eternal

89

destiny.   Here you determine your heaven
or hell.   Here settles there.   Here are you
building for eternity."

Are we redeeming the time?   Are we
earnestly buying up every opportunity for
soul-culture and for God's glory?   How
are these golden hours slipping by,—
freighted with the fruits of consecrated living, or are they only vain, empty, idle air-
bubbles?

A condemned man was told that his
supply of water would measure the time of
his reprieve.   Do you blame him for scru-
pulously saving every drop or using it as if
it were liquid gold?

Are we thoughtful concerning time,
reckoning only upon the present moment as
ours?   The next one may find us in the
presence of God.   The apostles repeatedly
urge time's shortness as an argument for
instant decision or immediate obedience.

Jesus had ever before him the end of his
earthly mission, and his motto was, "I
must work the works of him that sent me;
the night cometh, when no man can work."
To the faithful toiler the coming of the
night will not mean gloom or darkness, but
the rest which cometh after work.   Paul

could say, "I have finished my course."
But that was only an echo of the Master's
triumphant words, "I have finished the
work which thou gavest me to do." But
what a night it will be for those who have
squandered time, and have idled away their
moments! The man without a wedding-
garment simply neglected to do what he
ought to have done when he had the time.
Then it was too late.

Time, next to character, is the most valu-
able element in life, for it is our portion of
eternity, loaned to us, in which we are to
prepare for all eternity. God's great "NOW"
is ringing in our ears. Every impulse to a
better, more faithful life, every stirring
within us toward God and eternity, is the
Holy Spirit drawing us away from the en-
tanglements of earth into the reality of
eternity. In the quiet hour, when we are
conscious of unseen realities, when we are
thoughtful, we can best learn the value of
time. What does all this indifference mean?
Simply that men do not believe God's
Word. They are not much interested in
the building of characters which shall out-
last the stars. The only inevitable outcome
of a Christless here is a Christless eternity.

Some day, in the hushed and waiting chamber, the world will seem very small, and eternity very near. The hour-glass will hold but a few grains of the golden sand. What then? An infidel cried out at such a time, "I am about to take a leap into the dark."

But listen to David's song, "Though I walk through the valley of the shadow of death, thou art with me." Listen to Paul, "I have a desire to depart, and to be with Christ." But, best of all, hear the words of the blessed Saviour, "If a man keep my saying, he shall never see death." Like the absent son, away from home for a long time, who comes back again, and has eyes only for the loved ones, so the disciple, looking to Jesus, will pass the shadows and stand upon the eternal shores of glory. So shall he ever be with his Lord, and the work of grace and time shall outshine the ages. Blessed Father, teach me so to number my days that I may apply my heart unto wisdom.

THE LENS OF PURITY.

Blessed are the pure in heart, for they shall see God.
—*Matt.* 5 : 8.

THERE is a legend that the angels ring a sweet-toned bell at twilight, but only those whose hearts are free from sin and passion can hear it. Blessed are the pure in heart, for they shall hear the music of heaven.

So there is also a vision of heaven which comes only to the pure-hearted. The vision of God is gathering around us just as the chariots and armies of heaven encamped upon Dothan's plains and hills.

God can be seen in life's sunshine and shadow. His presence is felt amid the toils and respites of service. His dear hand can be recognized, leading to still waters or across turbulent waves. He comes in the early morning hour, and blesses the beginning of the day. He abides with us at evening, and watches over us through the night.

But who can see? The natural man cannot know the things of God, because they are spiritually discerned. He who would see the things of God must be in the Spirit. If you would meet God, you must first meet his conditions for seeing. Jesus was not seen by the multitudes after his resurrection because henceforth the spiritual kingdom could be only spiritually discerned.

Intellect is a mighty power. It can harness the material forces. It can make wind and wave do its bidding. It sends its messages by the flash of the lightning. It can track the stars and mark the pathway of the planets. But it cannot find or see God. The finest microscope or the longest telescope cannot discover him. What is denied to imperial intellect is given to simple faith, but simple faith must look through a pure heart.

> " Blind unbelief is sure to err
> 　　And scan his work in vain;
> 　God is his own interpreter,
> 　　And he will make it plain."

The heart burdened with unforgiven sin, or tarnished with the world's life, or obscured by unbelief, cannot see the heavenly vision. God can do nothing for an impure heart unless he first cleanse it. The power that cleanses also removes the blindness. "Once I was blind ; now I can see."

The blessing of the pure heart is the beginning of fellowship with the pure and holy God. Faith and purity offer to God a life in which he can dwell.

> " Near, so very near to God,
> Nearer I cannot be.
> For in the person of his Son
> I am as near as he."

As the gospel, which came from above, is first pure, then peaceable, so our hearts must first be pure before we can have the peace of God's presence. O that we might long more and more to be children of the pure heart and open vision, hating sin and striving to live clean, holy lives, and to keep ourselves unspotted from the world! We can see God only as the lenses of faith are cleansed and kept clean by obedience. Blessed are the pure-hearted, for they shall discern the Lord, until at last they shall see him eye to eye and face to face.

My soul, hast thou heard the voice of God, and yet thou canst not see him ? The fault lies wholly with thee. Thou canst not see, because thou art wilful, impure, disobedient, and the vision is withheld. Offer up thy prayer, "Lord, cleanse me that I may see." Keep thyself pure, and thou shalt see.

And dost thou ask, "How may I retain the vision of God?" Thou canst not hold it by a dreamy, serviceless life. "He that hath seen me hath seen the Father," said Jesus. If thou wouldst retain the vision, thou must obey his word and do his will. Only those who work with him can walk with him. The burning heart will manifest the fellowship of Christ as thou dost go forth in his name to tell to others the blessing and the gospel of the pure heart. Make haste and do his bidding, and verily on the King's highway thou shalt see the King in all his beauty.

Blessed Father, I crave the precious vision of thyself, that my restless life might be quieted in thy presence. Sanctify my heart, and make me pure, that I may see thee and rejoice in thy fellowship. Deepen my pure life, that I may see the highest vision.

God's Vigilance.

He that toucheth you toucheth the apple of his eye.—
Zech. 2: 8.

HAT God has said concerning his care of Zion applies to every member of Zion. It is wonderful how patiently God seeks to impress upon our reluctant minds the ministry of his love, which he extends to his children in all the details of life. Here he uses the eye as the object-lesson to teach us the lesson of his loving providence. "He that toucheth you toucheth the apple of his eye."

How marvellous an organ the eye is, perfect in its mechanism, in its protection, and in its sensitiveness! It is so finely set that its use comes to us almost unconsciously. It is so delicate that God has placed the most sensitive and alert sentinels to watch over its safety and welfare. The slightest interference with its functions, the smallest foreign particle, is at once felt and known.

97

Touch the apple of the eye, and the whole physical organism is aware of it.

This is the object-lesson to teach us the vigilance of God in our behalf. In this world we are lifted into fellowship with God through faith in his Son. But evil forces are constantly around us. We cannot hope to escape the enmity of the world or the temptations of the evil one. If we are the friends of God, the enmity of the world will increase. Nor are we able, single-handed, to cope with the powers of evil. This is our sure defence. These hostile forces may surge upon us up to a certain limit, and our fears may perhaps see the plains filled with enemies. But our divine Protector stands between us and the danger, and challenges the enemy: "Go no farther. He that toucheth one of the least of these toucheth the apple of mine eye. These are my children, and I throw around them the protection of my omnipotence." Above and around the armies of the plains are the chariots and the legions of heaven. When God is on our side, alert, vigilant, almighty, who can prevail against us?

This object-lesson also suggests our union with God. Sin separates from God. Evil drives us into the wilderness of temptation. But God loves, and his love has searched us out; for we are as dear to him as the apple of his eye. He brings us back again to his heart, and we are no longer prodigals, but children of his household. "He that is joined unto the Lord is one spirit." We are bound up in the same bundle of life with our Lord.

This also suggests the value which God puts upon his children. We are precious in his sight. He is concerned about our welfare. He loves to guard us and protect us.

This also suggests his loving care. "God will take care of you; be not afraid." He will not permit sorrow to crush you. Though the waters of affliction come over you, they shall not overwhelm you. David prayed very earnestly, "Keep me as the apple of the eye," and afterward, out of the experience of fulfilled promises, he could have sung, "He kept me, he kept me as the apple of his eye."

This also suggests divine sympathy. As the eye is intensely sensitive, and responds to the slightest touch, so God not only thinks of us, but he answers our faintest cry; he knows our frame, and he will respond to

the cry of danger and need. He identifies
the humblest soul with his infinite wisdom,
"I am with you, saith the Lord."

Blessed Father, thou hast put thy infinite
value upon our poor human lives. Thou
dost say to all adverse forces, "He that
toucheth this child of mine toucheth the
apple of mine eye." We thank thee for thy
great vigilance. Help us to live so close to
thee that thy eye may not only guard us,
but also guide us. Give us grace to reach
up more and more into the eternal security
of thy omnipotent vigilance. Help us to be
so sensitive to thy voice and will that we
may respond to every word of thine. Keep
us, for we cannot keep ourselves, and deliver us from all evil, until at last, with shining soul and perfect heart, we shall live
with thee in the bright mansions beyond the
skies.

IN GOD WE TRUST.

Blessed are all they that put their trust in him.—*Ps.*
2: 12.

AVID'S confidence expressed itself in this triumphant confession: "O my God, I trust in thee." Job indicated the depth of his trust by exclaiming, "Though he slay me, yet will I trust in him." Trust is the genuine currency in the kingdom of heaven.

Our life is in God. In him we move and have our being. In him we may also trust. As the mountains encircled the Holy City, so his presence is round about us, and our eyes of faith may see him.

Faith opens the door of the heart; love welcomes the Lord, and crowns him King; and trust bids him remain as the abiding guest of the life. His presence is real to us, because we are his children and he has given us the Spirit of his Son, who teaches us to say, "Abba, Father."

A little child was walking with a grown friend. As she wandered along, she plucked a beautiful flower. She gazed into its face with such wistfulness that he asked, "My dear, what does it look like?" She raised her sweet face until the light of it caught his eye, and then she said so reverently, "Why, it looks like God." There was in her heart, in some measure, the consciousness of God's presence.

It is not God's almightiness that brings the peace of trust, but his fatherliness that inspires love and confidence. We go to the humblest home blessed with love, and we see in the father-love or the mother-love the precious counterpart of God's love for us.

We are not asked to fathom its infinity or to understand its eternity. Surely a child can receive and return love without understanding it. Trust, then, is the placing of ourselves so near God that we may love him more and more, and share in his plans for us as children take some part in the plans of their parents. Obedience is the door that opens into privilege. If we obey, all things are possible. If we disobey, we shall lose many things.

Perhaps some weary soul, battling with doubt, conscious of only uttering self, is saying: "I wish that I could know just what to do, to trust more. I am like a child, who knows a few rudiments, and repeats them over and over again without getting any farther."

"I being in the way, the Lord led me." With open heart and candid mind, come to the Word, receive its message as you would a pressing invitation from your dearest friend, by believing what the Word has said. Then trust God because he has spoken to you, and you will grow in your trust as you grow in your love for him.

An artist long sought a piece of fine sandalwood out of which to carve a Madonna. He was about to give up his search, when in a dream he was bidden to carve his masterpiece out of a block of common oak wood destined for the fire. Many of us are waiting for some great experience, which shall lift us into greater trust. The true method is simply to believe what God has spoken and take him at his word.

Dear Father, thou knowest all about me. Draw me by the cords of love so close to thee that in thy presence I might grow in trust. Forgive me for doubting thee, and disclose thyself to me, that my little faith may increase to implicit confidence.

I thank thee that my soul is opening more
and more to the Spirit's indwelling. Sweep
thy light into every corner of my heart, that
I might see my life as thou seest it, and
mark the shining way before it.

Not with the eye of sense, but with the
obedience of trust, may I faithfully follow
my Jesus wherever he leads and whenever
his dear voice calls. My faith looks up to
thee, my blessed Father. I am thy property,
thy child. I do trust thee.

"Take my lips, and speak through them.
Take my mind, and think through it. Take
my heart, and set it on fire with love's sacred flame."

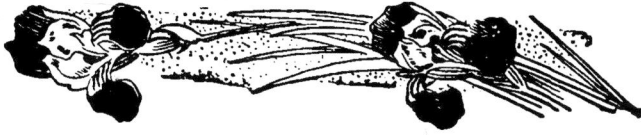

The Lost Chord.

Wilt thou not revive us again: that thy people may rejoice in thee?—*Ps.* 85 : 6.

" Come Holy Spirit, heavenly Dove,
 With all thy quickening powers;
Kindle a flame of sacred love
 In these cold hearts of ours."

WHAT is our utmost and pressing need to-day? It is not material comforts, not greater prosperity, not opportunity to serve, not more forms in which to express our worship. We have all the appointments. But God is Spirit, and they who worship him must worship in spirit and in truth. Deep down in the Christian heart there is an intense longing for something more permanent and enduring, an intuition which rises above the material, and hungers for God. There is always danger that the material may usurp the place of the spiritual in the life. It can never take its place, but it can hem it in and stifle its expression. The psalmist felt this. Surrounded by royalty and wealth, he cried out, "O Lord, revive me, lest these things overwhelm my soul." We are always in danger of becoming like the earth-clods at our feet. The ear becomes dull, the light of faith is dimmed, the soul becomes sordid. "O Lord, send thy life into my poor spasmodic living. Send thy light into my flickering dimness."

Why can we not be constant and firm in our religious life? Why cannot the waters of salvation run through the channels with steady flow? Simply because we are spasmodic in our obedience. How much we are like our local rivers, now almost dry, and then overflowing their banks, hurrying to the sea, only to meet the ebb and the flow of the ocean.

But this is not God's plan for our lives. O that we might be constant and willing in the day of his power! You remember the story of the lost chord. A musician sat at the organ, wearied with life's problems. His fingers, wandering over the keys, suddenly struck a chord of music that thrilled him. It was like the sound of heaven's great "Amen." The discord of his life gave way to the celestial harmony. And then the sound died away, and the old pain came back. He sought in vain for that chord, and at last, almost in despair, he said, "It may be that only in heaven I shall hear that grand Amen."

Is this to be the history of our soul-life? Must we wait until then to get our hearts in tune with the Infinite? The blessed Father is willing to-day to tune our hearts to his harmony if we will be willing instruments in his hand. The soul surrendered to him will find its truest harmony in doing the divine will.

A poor invalid sitting in the gloaming said, "O, I wish that some master musician would play this pain out of my tired life." A stranger was passing the window, and heard the complaint. He quietly entered the room, and sat down at the open piano. The stars were lighting the pathway of the skies, and the full round moon cast its silver beams athwart the room. The stranger began to play. The music was entrancing, as if the melody of heaven had fallen upon the earth, and the sweet strains carried away the pain and the discontent from out the heart of the invalid. It was Beethoven improvising his marvellously sweet "Moonlight Sonata."

My soul, why art thou not rejoicing in the joy of thy salvation? Art thou shut in within narrow limits, or racked with care and pain, saying, "O that some master hand would put music into my heart in place of this world's jangle and discord!" Art thou sighing for the joy which thou didst have, but which thou hast lost? There is only One who can and will revive thee until thou canst rejoice. He stands knocking at thy door. He wants to come in. He wants to pour the music of heaven into thy life. Unbar the door. Open it wide. Make room for him. Gather up the energy of thy faith, and say: "Blessed Master, sweep the keys of my heart, and turn all this discord into thy blest harmony. Tune the harp of my soul. Make me constant in my praise, so that I may daily sing my hymn of joy. Help me to live a steadied life of trust. Always forward, never backward, help me to keep up with thee in life's daily walk and fellowship with thee."

> "My burdens, Lord, I bring to thee;
> O change them into songs for me.
> No other place heart-strength affords,
> My King of kings, my Lord of lords."

The Greater Works.

He that believeth on me, the works that I do shall he do also; and greater works than these shall he do, because I go unto my Father.—*John* 14 : 12.

JESUS CHRIST speaks with authority. The people who heard him were moved by the power of his spoken word. Peter was right; "Lord, to whom shall we go? Thou hast the words of eternal life."

He is more than a teacher of truth. He is the reservoir and the fountain. " I speak that which I do know, and testify that which I have seen." His words were omnipotent. He spoke, and the storm hushed itself to sleep. He spoke, and deaf, dull ears heard with gladness. He spoke, and sightless eyes turned, lighted with love, to meet his face. He spoke, and the sepulchred dead arose to meet the Lord of life.

His works were also omnipotent. His miracles were the works of God. He commanded the winds to be still. He walked upon the waters, and turned water into

109

wine. He touched leprosy and it fled. He fed the hungry thousands, and brought returning health to unnumbered sick folk.

"The works that I do shall ye do also." The early disciples, receiving the Holy Spirit, did perform these works. Peter and John met the cripple at the Beautiful Gate, and commanded him to rise. The sick and the afflicted came to the disciples as they did to the Master, and in the name of Jesus mighty deeds were performed.

But the time came when the kingdom of the greater works was ushered in, for Jesus also said, "Greater works than these shall ye do." The time came when the Kingdom was lifted out of the tangible and seen into the unseen kingdom of spiritual ideals and of faith unaided by the physical eye. To-day we are in the midst of the greater works. Greater than the opening of blind eyes is it to open spiritual eyes, for the eyes of sense must sooner or later be closed in the darkness of death. It was great to feed five thousand with the bread that multiplied in the Saviour's hand, but infinitely greater is it to feed hungry souls with the bread of life so that they shall hunger no more. It was great to walk on the water, but it is much greater to lead faltering foot-steps to the feet of Jesus. It was great to raise the dead, but it is infinitely greater to lead the soul to Jesus, who said, "If a man keep my saying, he shall never see death."

This is the meaning of the greater works. "Ye are my friends, if ye do whatsoever I command you." The clear call of the Master to his service commissions us to enter upon this largest field of the spiritual king-dom. We are the representatives of Christ upon this earth. Through us the messages of God are conveyed to the souls of men and women. How responsible a position we occupy! We ought to accept every opportunity for the strengthening of soul and spirit in order that we may resolutely meet the demands of the Kingdom. Are we consecrated to the holy task? We can do these greater works, because Jesus has ascended to the supreme place of power, and has sent to us the Spirit, who will give us our special ordination for service. "Be-cause ye are sons, God hath sent forth the Spirit of his Son" into our hearts and lives, that we might continue the service of the greater Son upon this earth.

Blessed Father, teach us ever to remember

that thou wilt fill our empty chalices to the brim only as we hold them still and quiet before thee. Prepare our hearts in the quiet hour for the practical and urgent duties of the busy hour. Deeper yet may thy Spirit press into our souls the enduement of thy great power.

We are such ready hearers and such tardy doers of thy Word! Thou dost work so patiently with us, in order that thou mightest lead us into active partnership with the great mission of thy Son. We long for thy glory, but we are reluctant to tread the rugged pathway of sincere and unfailing service which leads up to it. Forgive us for being timid, and fill us with a holy ambition to grasp firm hold of thy great plans, that we might truly and courageously live the life more abundant, and be faithful disciples of the greater works.

A Threefold Ministry.

But thou, O Lord, art a shield about me; my glory, and the lifter up of mine head.—*Ps.* 3 : 3.

AVID'S song grew out of the experience of his soul in the hour of his peril, when the rebellion of his son menaced him with disaster. His trust in God found expression in this hymn, in which he praises God for a threefold ministry.

1. "Thou art a shield about me." Jehovah said to Abram, "Fear not, I am thy shield." What an omnipotent weapon of defence, which the enemy's dart cannot penetrate! God is our fortress behind which we may hide. But here he is our shield behind which we may fight. The shield is an alert weapon in warfare. Little do we know concerning the unseen forces of evil which oppose us, but God himself is the shield round about us, which can instantly be turned toward the point of attack.

My soul, make much of thy shield. Fight the good fight of faith, and fear not, for the

powers for thee are much greater than those
against thee.   But thou must fight if thou
wouldst obtain the victory.   Thou must
link thy little strength with the omnipotence
of thy shield.

2. "My glory."   The glory of earth's
honor is empty and vain.   The glory of
God is everlasting.   The Holy One that in-
habits eternity is also willing to dwell in the
humblest human heart.   The world may
say, "Who are you? what have you done
to deserve so great honor that God dwells
with you?"   We may safely reply, "I am
nothing, I have done nothing, I deserve
nothing; but God loves me and dwells with
me because I am a child of his and he is my
glory."   As a sunbeam is only an infinitesi-
mal gleam of the sun, yet it can reflect the
glory of the king of day; so the humblest
life may receive and reflect God's glory.
As a dewdrop lying unseen on a rose's
petal may be small, yet in its crystal face it
can retain and reflect the colors of the rainbow, and carry to the heart of the rose the
glory of the skies, so the humblest life may
catch the gleams of God's glory and be an
angel of light to other lives.

My soul, be of good courage.   The world

may not honor thee, but God will crown thee with his mercy. The fashion of the world passeth away, but God will enrich thee forever. As the flowers abide in the sunshine, so keep in the sunshine of God's love, and thou wilt surely behold and share in the glory of the Father.

3. "The lifter up of mine head." God sheds the light of his face upon us. But here he will lift up the face. What does it mean? He will lift up the head under the weight of trials, so that we shall not be discouraged. He will take from us the sense of guilt for past offences, and restore to us the joy of salvation. The child who has been disobedient is conscious of his guilt. He withdraws to a corner, where he may somehow hide the shame written on his face. The father has heard the confession of the child's wrongdoing, and has said, "My child, I forgive you." But the child hangs his head. Something more is needed to bring back the sunshine. The father draws near, and with his loving hand he lifts up the guilt-stricken face into the light and the love of his own smiling face and favor, and kisses the troubled brow. The restoration is complete. So God deals with

us. Disobedience sends us into the shadows of conscious guilt. We have lost the joy, the light of his presence. He forgives us, and he restores our souls by lifting up the face into the light of his blessed countenance; and, as we look up, we catch the message of love beaming in his eye.

My soul, why art thou cast down? Why dost thou hide thy face in the shadows? Thou canst not look up, because thou hast grieved the Father-heart with thy disobedience and wilfulness. Confess thy wrongdoing. God is so willing to forgive. The shadow still clings to thee. See, the blessed Hand is stretched out. Love divine lifts thy face out of the clouds into the glory of God's presence, until it catches the light of an eternal sunrise. Now thou canst sing with all thine heart,

> " When Jesus shows his smiling face,
> There is sunshine in my soul."

HEART-HYMNS.

The Lord was ready to save me; therefore we will sing my songs.—*Isa.* 38: 20.

GOD heard Hezekiah's prayer, and gave him back his health again. The king did not rebel against Providence in his sickness unto death, but he did pray most fervently for restoration, and God was ready to heal him.

The heart which feels the touch of infinite power is also awakened to a sense of gratitude and rejoicing. Hezekiah expressed his joy over answered prayer in this hymn of praise.

> " The Lord was ready to save me,
>   Therefore we will sing my songs,
>   To the stringed instruments,
>   All the days of our life,
>   In the house of the Lord."

Let us heartily thank God for a gospel that can be sung, the very music of which, expressed in glad tidings, stirs the heart.

The ministry of hymns has been a great blessing in the progress of God's kingdom.

The history of the Christian life can be written in the songs of Zion. The apostle speaks of singing in the heart and making melody unto the Lord. The true hymn is the language of the heart.

Next to hiding God's Word in the heart, these precious hymns, committed to memory, have been a sweet and tender blessing to the Christian pilgrim. Many an aged saint has been comforted and helped by such ministry of hymn and music.

The hymns learned in youth come back again in old age laden with precious memories and deep experiences. Thank God for a gospel that sings itself into our daily lives, and that bids us sing away sorrow and care. Sin has no hymns. Evil does not care to sing. A man steeped in iniquity has little heart to sing the songs of home; yet how often the memory of a mother's hymn has touched the prodigal's heart, and brought the tears of sorrow and repentance!

David thanked God for hymns which he could sing in the night. Instead of spending sleepless nights of anxiety and worriment, he made the dark hours bright with music and with song, recalling God's goodness and mercy to him. No matter how dark our experiences may be, no matter how deep the night may sink into our lives, we can sing our hymn and rejoice in the Lord. "My mouth shall praise thee with joyful lips, when I remember thee." There are times when we cannot help singing, for God's sunshine is so bright. "O happy day that fixed my choice!" Or we are perhaps burdened with a great load of care, and our hearts are wounded. "Earth has no sorrows that heaven cannot heal." We are in the storms of life. "Jesus, Lover of my soul."

Perhaps we are harassed by a multitude of trials or changes, and we wonder what it all means. "Thou who changest not, abide with me."

We may be standing at the rim of a new-made grave, and we are thinking of buried hopes and emptied hearts. "Nearer, my God, to thee."

Thus, if our hearts are in tune with the Infinite, the hymns of Zion will minister balm and comfort to our souls.

Some one has said that the sweetest music which he ever heard came from the lips and the heart of an old slave. He was travelling through the pine groves of the

South.   At a little distance from him he saw
a poor hut, and before it a woman at her
work was singing this heart-hymn :—

"Nobody knows the joys I have; nobody knows but
Jesus."

There was triumph and gladness in every
tone of her voice.

Then there was a pause, and in a minor
key she put her sorrow in every word.
"Nobody knows the sorrows I have; nobody knows but Jesus."

Yes, blessed Saviour, thou dost know all.
Whether our hearts are happy or sad, we
love to sing of thee and to thee.   We rejoice that thou art so near us that even in
our singing thou canst hear our prayers or
our vows.   Help us to translate our hymns
into experience, and to be sincere singers.
We receive courage and comfort from the
hymns of Zion because thou dost put thy
melody into our souls.   Thou dost set our
lives to the music of thy love.   Thou dost
transpose our trials and weariness into songs
and hymns.

GOD'S SUMMITS.

Come up hither, and I will shew thee things which must be hereafter.—*Rev.* 4: 1.

E who would see the spiritual kingdom must himself be Spirit-filled. John looked into the opened heaven, and saw the vision of the unseen, because he lived so near its gates. Mystery un'olds itself, the nearer we approach it, in spiritual attainment. What John saw, he knew that he would reach some day. God can never do anything for a man who is spiritually blind, unless he open his eyes. God will reveal nothing to a man who wants to be blind.

The scope of the vision is in proportion to the outreach of the soul. The place is not a barrier. Christ can make a desert glow as a morning sunrise, when he comes and reveals himself. Picture John's lonely exile life on Patmos. There was nothing helpful or pleasing on the cold, bleak shores of that barren island. But heaven touched it, and there was glory everywhere. The life, not the place, determines the vision. Wherever you are, if it is a God-appointed place, you may see the vision which will transfigure the lowliest toil and service. God's glory will lift the life above its material environment, and lead the soul up into the divine altitude.

John immediately responded to the coming of the Spirit. The power that exalts the vision also fills the soul. The nearer we get to the pure summits of God, the deeper we shall breathe in the inspiration of his presence. "Mountaineers are always freemen." "If the Son shall make you free, ye shall be free indeed." If we are risen with Christ, we can also ascend with him to the summit privileges of God's children. May we be among his true freemen, longing to live the higher life, because we are deeply rooted and grounded in the life and the love of God.

Hawthorne's allegory of the Stone Face has a helpful message. The young man into whose soul the prophecy entered so deeply gazed upon the great Stone Face, and longed for the coming of the pure and noble man. In a quiet way he translated his ideals into humble and unselfish service until at last he himself became the fulfilment of the local prophecy.

Thank God, we have not a stone face, into whose lustreless eyes we must gaze. Thank God, we can see Jesus, in whose blessed face shines the glory light of God. As we look into his face, and as we serve him unselfishly and unswervingly, we shall not only reflect his image, but we shall be more and more conformed to his likeness.

How much we need the vision of the face divine, in the midst of our daily toils ! We need the transfiguration glory of the summit to keep us true and faithful amid the arduous tasks in the valley. We need the atmosphere of the exalted altitude to help us breathe as we labor in the stifling regions of misery and sin.

The summit vision will transfigure the whole life. The soul's horizon is completely changed when it accepts God's invitation, " Come up and live with me."

Dannecker, the great sculptor, carved his vision of Christ into Carrara marble. The emperor ordered a statue of Venus for the Louvre. Dannecker replied: " Sire, I cannot. A man who has seen Christ would commit sacrilege if he should employ his art in the carving of a pagan goddess. My art is henceforth a consecrated thing."

My soul, hast thou seen Christ? Alone with thy God, hast thou heard his voice, "Come up and live with me, and I will show you things which must be hereafter"? Art thou pressing toward the summits of God? Remember that he will keep thee on the heights if thou art wholly consecrated to him. Living or dying, art thou the Lord's? Then thou canst also say: "I have pledged myself to the Lord. Henceforth my life is a consecrated living with my God." As Moses lifted up his eyes from Pisgah's summit, and saw the promised land before him, so mayest thou, from God's great summit, see the King in his beauty and behold the land of far distance.

"So the purer life grows nigher every year.
And its morning star climbs higher every year.
And earth's hold on us grows slighter,
And the heavy burdens lighter,
And the dawn immortal brighter every year."

A Consecration Hymn.

"Jesus, my King, with thorn-crowned brow,
  O let thy Spirit fill me now.
  In faith I kneel before thy cross;
  All earthly things I count but dross.

"Yes, Lord, I hear thy voice of love
  That draws my soul to thee above.
  For strength I ask, to follow thee
  Where'er by faith thy hand I see.

"I give myself, my time, my all;
  In worship at thy feet I fall.
  Then bid me rise to service new,
  Whate'er there is for me to do.

"I will obey thy voice divine,
  And calmly place my hand in thine;
  I'll follow thee with joyful heart,
  Where'er I can thy Word impart.

"My burdens, Lord, I bring to thee;
  O, change them into songs for me.
  No other place heart-strength affords,
  My King of kings, my Lord of lords."

Made in United States
North Haven, CT
20 October 2024

59196121R00081